a
storm
encountered

alexis jade petri

You:
The storm that rolled in…

He was my first love,
and like all first loves it was sudden,
impeding,
and appeared with all the luster of the moon.
As time went by and this love was not allowed to last,
I clung to it
with the strength I should have been clinging to myself.
The detaching had to begin.
First my limbs from his,
then miles,
and now memories.
Memories tangled in with tears
and the looming realization that he is not all there is,
and that perhaps I measured the strength of my love for him
by the intensity of pain I experienced.
Perhaps I should have loosened my grip long ago,
but I only knew how to nurture,
never to kill.
Now I see,
there are weeds in our garden
we can't water along with the flowers...
hoping to cause growth,
but ultimately killing the beauty therein.

Just as ethereally as you entered my world, did you leave...
with what felt like all smoke and mirrors,
I wondered in which of your words or kisses
was there ever any truth.
In attempts at obtaining closure,
I grabbed your hands
and tried to patch my heart's holes with them...
the same hands that pierced.
Sweetly
and helplessly unaware of your inability to bring such healing,
I've reached for you time and again.
I've engaged in every one of your games
and started a few myself.
All in what hopes?
That you would lie with me again only so I could push away
the moment I'm pulled close?
You see,
I'm not intimate by nature,
and you've never known of the love I carry.
Surely you would have been frightened to know
the depth of what I felt,
and still feel to my dismay.
So here I am,
saying hello when I intended much more,
and goodbye,
when it was tears I ached to release.

And so I realized that I've been scared…
That word doesn't escape my lips easily,
but nothing has struck more fear into my heart
than the realization that I've loved you
more fiercely than I thought possible.
You melted my wall of ice with your warm stare,
and here I am,
still trying to freeze it over…

Please tell me you don't miss me in the slightest
so I'll know there's hope for me too...

After all this time I'm still uncertain of what you wanted.
Reminding myself that it wasn't in hopes of love,
as that is something you had already obtained.
But if it was just my skin you wanted,
would you have waited like you did?
And if it was only momentary,
why take such risks?
I'm no longer seeking answers from you
because I don't need them,
and my life no longer aches for you to take up space in it.
I do ponder at times though,
why I was the one you chose to victimize under the disguise of
pursuit
and
passion.
Two things I knew little about,
and you,
like a stained glass window,
beautifully distorted my view of both.

You planted a doubt within me,
making it hard for me to recognize at first,
but now I see clearly.
This growing doubt,
the belief that without you here I can't be fully happy,
and that perhaps I might never be able to escape
this home you've built within me.
Spreading your blood through my veins,
and embedding your touch beneath my skin.
This doubt it grew and took root,
subtly amongst all the hope,
making itself more evident with time.
But you see,
doubtful I am not,
nor am I weak.
And though I may have loved you with a passion
I did not think possible,
just as easily can I give that to another if I so desire.
So while it will take time and intention,
I will escape you just fine,
and uproot this doubt with my bear hands if I must.
Because you were too cowardly
to love with the strength that was needed,
and still I invited you in.
This time around though,
I'm learning to lock my doors at night,
and fill the hallways with my own paintings…

As much of you as I shake from memory,
there is always this desire for your laughter…
that maybe it would reside in my chest,
living there keeping it full.
And when I laugh,
yours would embrace it,
filling all the empty spaces where words are never enough.

Even in the moments I felt a fierce rage toward you,
I could never scorn your laughter…

You eloquently put on your armor
and spoke words of valor in response to my questions,
but all along you were fighting for what you wanted,
never what I deserved…

What did it look like to love him?
It looked like the easiest thing in the world...
But what it felt like...
it felt like swimming against the current
toward a shore that didn't exist.

Sometimes I think I'm always telling the same story
about you...
how you climbed on my roof and started removing shingles.
But with each shingle comes a different story.
A different tale of how you started tearing them away
thinking you were helping me see the sun more clearly...
and I thought you were too.
When in reality,
you were only exposing me to the storm...
the storm that was falling for you.
And I hope you know that I don't blame you completely,
because I was the one who let you up there.
I danced with your words instead of hearing your intentions.

You won't diminish me.
Not having you around never made me less of a person.
So it's up to me,
I suppose,
whether I'll let your absence feel like
neglect
or
freedom.

Why do I still romanticize you in my dreams,
when you're the monster in my closet...

I've tried to humanize you and soften your sharp edges
because it is in my nature,
but I sit here now questioning it all.
Those edges I so gently tried to shape
have now cut me and her.
Her,
who loved you long before I did,
and perhaps held your hands when they were softer...
before they held questions that calloused them,
and a hurt that forced their grip.
I will always hope for your healing,
and that you find whatever you were looking for in me,
inside of yourself.
And as much as I wanted to,
I can't quiet your demons,
and you can't drown them out.
Face them you must,
calloused hands and all,
still holding shards of the broken hearts you created.

Your letter sits folded in a book by my bed.
Tear stained and memorized.
Although when I look back on it,
I see how little you knew of me…
repeating things I've said about myself back to me,
but never really scratching the surface.
And maybe that's because we didn't have much time,
or because you didn't really care to.
"Remember,"
you said,
"your greatest fear is not becoming the woman
you want to be,"
and you were right.
Now maybe what that means to me
is never hurting someone the way you hurt me…
making me believe I could have you in some capacity
when I never could.
Never would.
And maybe never really wanted to,
if I ever had enough time to actually understand
what was happening inside me.
I really did just want to be close to you,
but distance and healing have some kind of connection
that is beckoning for my acknowledgment.

When I said I could fill books with what I feel,
it was not in a state of exaggeration.
Every emotion I never understood,
I've now felt all at once.
How you can love someone with the passion of a fire,
and still say goodbye to them
every time.
How you can idealize some form of purity,
and roll in the dirt that's been thrown at you.
Questioning everything I believed about
love and commitment,
choices,
truth,
and all that you involved me in,
yet I was not strong enough to say no a second time around.
While I spent so much time secretly hoping
you still clung to the thought of me the way I did for you,
I also wanted to find my own in this mess.
Find clarity amidst the disaster.
And you know what,
I'm still on that journey,
and there isn't room for you on that path...

It was never about me…
you wanted something
and I was naive enough to give it to you.
You drank in your selfishness
until you were drunk and careless.
I got in the car with you just in time for you to wreck it.
Now after all this time,
I'm still pulling the bits of glass from my heart.
Shard by shard,
being reminded of you with each extraction.

That specific day,
I wanted nothing more than to run away with you,
but instead you ran away from me.
In that crowded room
our eyes met for the first time in almost a year,
and when I turned my back for a moment,
you were gone.
Along with you and your briefcase
left my hopes of our ultimate collision.
It no longer exists.
All that remains now is an empty table where you sat,
and a room filled with faces and choices.
I felt the force of the door slamming behind you,
hitting me with a rush of sorrow and freedom
carried in one breeze.
I felt your release of me,
and it left me numb but eerily hopeful...

It won't always be about you.
This ache that lingers like the last bit of water
dripping from the faucet.
Wasting water,
and irritating the listener.
Your ghost has bathed in my tub for far too long now,
and I've yet to drain it,
hoping you would return.
But the dirt from your hands is not mine to keep,
it is no souvenir from your stay.
Like that slow drip,
it is slow to drain,
so I will be patient for your departure
just as I was for your arrival,
knowing that water eventually evaporates,
leaving behind the porcelain that was always there.

Do you see what you've done...
these skies you painted in two separate worlds,
trying to bask under both simultaneously.
You truly thought the hail wouldn't come for you
on both accounts?
That you could escape the wrath of the storm you stirred up...
well now it's come,
and here you stand with a choice.
You see I've loved you enough
to attempt to save you from this despair,
but I chose to paint my own skies and leave yours in my past.
And though I've been tempted with the desire
to return to your stars,
it has dawned on me,
their light was never true,
and their source an untrustworthy one.

I have something to say.
I've always had something to say.
You kissed me so forcefully
I swallowed the words I should have turned you away with.
Now don't you dare utter my name
as if the words mean something to your mouth.
And while you act as if water has carried away your troubles,
fires from all the years of extinguishing
are now burning fiercely in my eyes.
They look brighter and feel clearer,
no longer clouded by the smoke you conjured up
for the sole purpose of misguiding my sparks...
all so they wouldn't burn holes in your sleeve.
You saw them,
although not for all they could be,
only for what you could ignite with them.
Now I'm swimming through flames as if they were waves,
because after the hell you were so unaware that I suffered,
the shore is no longer home to me,
and my skin is much thicker without you underneath it.

You smile and move on with your life,
knowing so little of the pain you caused me.
I,
trying so hard to stay strong and steady,
never let on how deep the cuts...
how passionate the love.
But that matters now just as much as
the promises you've made...
little,
and pointless to hold on to.

Where are the things I considered to be whole…
the pieces I assumed I needed to carry?
They've moved through the space between you and I,
the space between the old skin I wore and the new,
the space between what is and what I dream of.
I'm trying to understand what fills that space now…
What am I waiting for?
What am I hoping for?
I am so whole without you,
yet trying to understand how I make my way
through that space now
without trying to pick up those pieces again…
the ones that stick to my hands so easily
and remind me of you.
But not with clarity.
It's a murky remembrance…
one that depicts you as more lovely and caring
than you ever were.

The cliff of our volatile love...
where I kept jumping,
knowing we couldn't stand on it long.
With each leap and goodbye you reached for my hand,
and I held on for dear life.
Every finger of ours intertwined was a different memory,
preventing me from releasing.
Wrestling with a fading love,
kept sustained by delusion.
We've waltzed in an endless dance of obsession,
swaying to nostalgia's song.
Crumbling ground,
dangling legs,
an imagined bliss.
Now I'll warn those who wander to the same ledge,
keep your eyes open dear,
reminiscing won't substitute reality.

How I've longed to reach for your hand,
while swatting it away in my mind.
In my dreams you linger,
while my subconscious wrestles with what it can cling to.
Every dream feeling like an encounter,
leaving me reeling upon awakening.
Whether I would rather push you out of reach,
or draw you to myself,
I am not altogether sure.
But amidst my confusion,
this I do know,
love cannot be diminished,
only redirected.

How is it that one scent can jolt you
with all the memories and heartache from a time long gone…
My perfume,
you had to clean from your car and jacket to forget,
but I never did.

Nowadays
I simply feel too tired to try and check up on you
like habits have driven me to.
Missing you drains more out of me
than a sleepless gloomy day.
Still I miss,
still I look,
but still I try to let go.
Tired eyes and achy hands you've caused,
but with every breath,
more rest will come to the parts of me that you awoke.

I feel the pressing need for rain...
downpour even.
Seeing the drops hit the glass window
draws out in me this restless need to be submersed.
A part of my soul hoping it will wash you from my skin,
as well as the longing for you altogether.
And though we live two separate lives under the same sky,
maybe the rain will wash you clean as well,
and the distance will heal what is left at our feet.
The remnants of what once was,
but can no longer be.

You made me fearless,
in a way.
Saying goodbye to you was the scariest thing I've ever done,
and I had to do it more than once.

There is a desert in my subconscious,
housing my questions and pain,
with endless dunes of dissonance
mounted upon the deception you laid.
There you stand in the center,
like a mirage I can see,
but collapsing upon my touch.
I've visited this place like a reflex,
wandering in a dazed state hoping to find waters
to wash away your sting.
After waiting in this desert for years,
the wind and rain finally came,
and I watched you disintegrate before me,
turning to the very sand you stood upon.
While the wind blew you through my hair and fingertips,
I looked on as you entered my palms for a moment
before I let the grains fall to my feet,
kicking through them in search of a stream to wash my hair.
I never did belong in the desert,
and you never belonged in love.

As if somehow time has forced events to occur
reversed in their order,
you and I are growing into strangers.
My memory strongly disagrees,
resurfacing moments as if we live within them now.
But the way we pass each other and look away,
it reminds me of busy streets filled with familiar faces
too guarded to connect…
people who knew each other once upon a time,
devoid of desires for rekindling.
Everything we've known of each other
has been swallowed by time,
and the title "strangers" suits us much better
than the lie that we are more.

The distance now feels closer than your hands ever did.

...how often we confuse a sentence with a book.

Me:
The house that withstood.

I am altogether unaware of what love does to a being.
How with each breath we inhale,
we must exhale as well,
and be subconsciously reminded of the pattern
of loving and letting go.
How that concept does not seem clear to a heart that believes
love should only hold on,
never release.
Is that the heart of love?
Can *lust* cause the aches within and lingering pain
I have believed love to cause?
Are the powers of both equally as strong,
yet different in their nature?
Can one remove the poison of either,
or both,
and walk enough distance to find freedom,
and an understanding of what separates the two?...

There was this music surrounding the journey
out of my youth...
no disharmony in the notes,
only spaces for more beauty.
I no longer looked at myself through a lens of expectation,
but searching.
Wading through my own self doubt and questions
to find the understanding that was embedded beneath.
I saw that my hopes had been scattered about
the landscape of my life,
but are now being gathered and housed...
housed for me to seek out and dwell in.
A place that is filled with harmonies saturated in both
hope
and
mystery.

What once sat on my floor was a girl who believed
the love she wouldn't have to settle for
didn't really exist.
Somehow she was ok with that,
and was set on discovering things for herself.
Seeing the extraordinary through her own set of eyes,
not needing another to dilute what her own heart
made of each moment.
She wanted to gather everyone close to herself,
but never be defined by an attachment
she would feel unable to sever.
Until he came…
he came with all the force of a shattering wind,
and she never expected it.
She spoke with cold words that covered her affection,
until she too was caught up in his hurricane.
Even after the rain stopped coming
and wind ceased to blow…
she still felt water under her feet,
and a breeze sweeping over her skin…

I'm desperately uninterested,
or fiercely fixated.
I don't totter that line.

I've bled different shades of holding on,
though under the impression I was letting go.
Painting my walls with each color,
and living within the mood they cast.
Do we eventually let go,
or simply convince ourselves that we have?...

She stood at an abandoned station
waiting for a train that wouldn't come,
when the wind reminded her
she had a beautiful life to live.
The wind whispered that there were people waiting outside
to watch her life unfold...
to get a glimpse of her splendor.
She was left with a choice that day,
to wait on the ghost train that would take her
to a distant place from her dreams,
or make her life a dreamy reality.
It was all in her.

I will keep answering yes
when the voice inside me asks if we will make it...
Yes dear voice,
we will.
We will love and learn and run free,
even though we hurt.
And when you ask me who we are,
I will answer you with truth instead of with woundedness.
I won't allow you to feel bad for yourself anymore dear one,
because all the things you've asked for
you have most certainly received.
And all the things you've lost
are because you gave them up.
The choice has been yours every time.
So take hold of what is rightfully yours,
and pride yourself in your choice
to let go of the things that hindered you.
You are leaping even though it feels like a crawl,
and the ponds in your life are really rivers,
flowing toward the places you want to go.
Keep following them,
and don't be distracted by those who are afraid to swim.
Be drawn and pulled by the power
that flows through the water,
and don't waver when it washes over your head for a bit.
Sometimes the prospect of drowning
reminds us how to swim.
You can't experience the current by simply looking on.
You weren't meant for safety sweet voice,
you were born to swim.

Full heart,
don't allow comparison to restrain your passion,
or plans to overwhelm your process.

In another realm entirely,
off behind the clouds,
lies some distant hope that pulls and sways
the waves within me,
mimicking the tides love affair with the sky.
To touch they are denied,
yet no dulling of their connection occurs.
With each gust the sky displays its passion,
and the water replies with her fierce tumultuous song.
Echoes of the age old love woven into our history,
and ever present throughout the years.
In my searching I won't waver,
and my doubt it will pass,
but to reach for such hope and chase it all my days,
let that be my journey...

I finally want to ride this wave.
The one that I've been content with rolling over my head
for as long as it has.
The saltwater is stinging my cuts,
and I'm not pretending they aren't there anymore.
I want to be above the water,
I want to ride it to wherever I end up.
I'm not concerned with the outcome,
only the strength it will take me to pull myself up
and kick away resistance.
I'm beautifully absorbed and determined in this moment.

This is a strange place for me to be,
can you tell?
This concept of staying put,
even if just for a moment.
I'm having to cultivate meaning
where there doesn't seem to be any,
and turn the disappointment around me to a living room.
Welcoming that which I apprehended,
and sitting down with it until I understand its cause.
It feels like intention.
Feels like a confrontation with my past and future
while we converse on this present ground.

Lately the physical brings to my attention
something stirring much deeper within,
and steadily forces itself to the center of my attention.
How outward bruises bring the thought to my mind
that I am not careful with myself...
limbs and words all the same.
It seems to me that carefulness is only absent
when we lack value for something.
How sweet this body that only you have,
and how clever this mind that only you can form
the thoughts and emotions within.
How present this laugh when your heart fills in a way
only it can,
and how bitter the heartbreak experienced by another
at its loss.
With bright eyes and that beautiful crooked smile,
you embrace the adventures ahead of you.
You are a modern wonder,
a breathtaking storm,
a chaotic ocean only revealing its depth
to those who dare swim in it.
Be careful with this sweet priceless frame,
for only you can.

You've always wanted to be free,
so stay free.
Loving him was your greatest slavery.
Remember heart,
how you felt when you had him.
You were so unhappy…
so distant.
His kisses were silencing you,
and his body lying on top of yours was crushing.
Remember it clearly now,
and don't let yourself be enslaved again.
Promise me that,
and let us heal.

Let it happen my love,
you feel it coming on like gentle butterflies
fluttering in the pit of your stomach.
But this time it feels different...
feels like falling out of love.
And though there is still the pressing desire for closeness,
there is now a background noise softly whispering
requests of distance.
Grant them that.
I think perhaps you made a vow to yourself
that you would wait for him,
and the very fibers of your being cling to that vow.
But he is not your story,
and you must pull your hopes from his hands now,
for he will not take care of them as you can.

I'm in this cloudy state of empty handedness.
Not in the way of lack,
but openness to embrace all that presents itself before me.
Do you know what I mean?
It's as if all the things I felt obligated to hold
have lost their weight,
and my fingers tingle with what feel like pings of expectation...
rendering me breathless
at the sight of my own incandescent wanderings.

She is effortlessly faithful to herself.
To the things that make her heart swell,
and the characteristics intrinsic to who she is.
Comfortable and satisfied with all that is her nature.
A believer in the truth of beauty being born and cultivated,
not bought or manufactured.
In love with her humanity,
and that of those around her.
Understanding,
aware,
observant,
content.
And unwilling to sacrifice any of this
on the altar of society's approval.

Now I hope you know that it's not the men you have loved,
but the miles you have traveled that made your mark.
Not the empty promises given you,
but the fullness of love you released.
You are so much more than the cracks…
you are the beauty that spilled out.

I've stood and looked on
at a finished product of myself in each season,
and with the changing of the leaves
she changes too.
She beckons me to just run a little further
that I would reach her outstretched hand,
but I never do…
not soon enough before her colors change shades…

-The poison of perfection

Whoever told you what love looked like?
Who broke your heart and made you believe
they had some kind of claim on it?
You have shared in beauty and shared in loss,
but never become less whole along that journey of exposure.
In losing your blinds
more light was let in.

I'm coming,
I promise I am…
running toward this tangible picture of all my hopes.
One that I'm chasing the moment I wake up,
only to begin again the next day.
And though I'm constantly being slowed to a crawl,
I'll still come.
On hands and knees,
reaching for this vision housed in my heart.
One of a restored view of our shattered hearts…
where they take the role of a compass,
urging us toward the love we were once too weary to chase.

So that's it then?
He wins?
Do you believe that if it's not him then it's no one?
The love you have to give is somehow
limited to what he receives?
Surely you must know there is more out there for you,
and you don't have to walk backwards to find it.

Isn't it funny how we let labels fall upon us like rain,
and assume we are a puddle?
When did we start becoming what we've been told we are?
"The storm itself"
suits you much better.

I was a silly naive girl
to think that falling in love with you would be an easy recovery,
but a foolish woman
to believe I won't rise above it.

In time my darling,
you will realize the love he gave
was not worth the pain he caused,
nor did he give either in equal proportion.
And when you see this,
you'll never let yourself crumble for such a love again.

I watched myself fight a battle
I never thought would come my way...
But there I was,
stunned by my own beautiful recovery.
Even now as it continues...